Symphonies of the heart

E.N. Gavani

BookLeaf
Publishing

India | USA | UK

Presentation by *BookLeaf Publishing*

Web: www.bookleafpub.com

E-mail: info@bookleafpub.com

ISBN: 9789360945824

First edition 2024

To Oliver and Gabriel,

*My little loves that teach me each day to
see the world with their big hearts.*

I love you this much,

(stretching my arms wide)

Mami

ACKNOWLEDGEMENT

A great thank you goes to my mom and my brother, who patiently listened to my blabbering for several days over our video calls about the ideas for this book, despite the 6-hour time change between us.
Thank you for being my best advisors and always encouraging me.

A special thank you goes to my mom.
Without her, I would have never taken such a leap of faith and this book would have never existed.

A huge thank you goes also to my husband. The labor of love included attending to a vivid toddler at night and changing a few more diapers than usual as I immersed in my own world with a pen and paper or brainstormed over my phone.
Thank you for loving me and always challenging me into becoming a better version of myself.

Love you all.

Dearest reader,

Thank you so much for choosing to read this book and for holding a piece of my heart in your gentle hands.
I hope your heart and soul find solace, joy, and encouragement through each verse that mine sang aloud.
This book is perceived to come to you as a symphony. Because just as a symphony, life has a certain ability to throw us around different experiences and tempos throughout the years, making music out of our heartbeat line.
The four chapters of this book are named after the four main family of instruments used in an orchestra, the percussions, the strings, the woodwinds and the brass.
Each instrumental-chapter is designed to convey a specific feeling and message.
So, sit back, get comfortable and I hope you enjoy the music.

Love,
E. N. Gavani

We are the composers of our own life's symphony.
 – E. N. Gavani

Contents

Prologue

Symphonies of the heart

A melody of emotions,
Notes written in a verse,
Symphonies of the heart,
Each line a universe.

– E.N. Gavani

Percussions of the Soul

If there is something special beneath the skies
meant for you,
rest assured that sooner or later it will come and
find you.
You only must have the courage to stay open and
receive it.

– E. N. Gavani

A moment in life

The journey you take,
when you embark away,
It never ceases, it never ends.
You keep on sailing,
searching for what has been missing.
All in vain.
For you have been parted.
Departed.
You've gone.

The places you left,
their pieces still within you,
Will begin to echo in your soul,
until no more sound will yield.
In place of what you left,
in place of what your soul seeks,
You will find yourself in pieces.
Memories scattered all around,
Until the boxes are wiped clean.
For you have trespassed.
Transgressed.
You have ignored.

And that earth that held your childhood steps,
And that air that caressed your years,
Will forget your essence,
all traces of you,
For you have stretched.
Streamed away.
You have withdrawn.

You start to question,
whether you're dead or alive,
If there is such a space,
a somewhere to belong.
Someplace to dream and hope will thrive,
To make new memories
and write a new song.
For you must accept.
Reconcile.
You must evolve.

To pilgrim, to wander,
a feeling indeed strange,
Writing anew,
on a blank new sheet,
You think you'd like
the commotion for a change,
Until the reality of it
comes slapping you on your cheek.

Wednesday, April 26th, 2023

You start to question, whether you're dead or
alive,
If there is such a space, a somewhere to belong.
Someplace to dream and hope will thrive,
To create new memories and write your new
song.

– E. N. Gavani

A simpler life

Somedays, I want to escape the madness of the
days,
Be stripped of every luxury I possess.
Away from the fluster of the modern world,
Leave it all behind, afar in a fog.

Somedays, I want to enjoy the peace and quiet
of nature,
Speak softly to my heart and my soul to nurture,
Exchange the riches for a slower simpler life,
Smell freshly baked bread and slice it with a
knife.

Somedays, I think I have done it all wrong,
For in another era, I wished that I belonged,
Dancing in the rain, forest bathing in the sun,
Forgetting everything and becoming undone.

Wednesday, March 13th, 2024

Undeserving world

I heard a nightingale sing aloud,
Ethereal music in the light of dawn.
A sole calling, no other birds to join,
A fragile voice in a tribe of foin.
Such strange to witness, a truth unreal,
A frightening realization, an inward scream.
And all the sudden I felt the pain of that poor little bird,
Singing his heart out to an undeserving cruel world.

Friday, March 15th, 2024

Voids

Your voids are your values.
Whatever you lack,
Wherever your void lays,
That is what you will value
And seek out the most.
For the void to be filled.
For what you lack to come to you.
For what you are missing to be found.
Let this journey of discovery bring indeed values
and not vices.

Monday, April 15th, 2024

I wandered lonely as a cloud

Ever heard a melody on the radio that brings you an explosion of feelings you want to put down into words? Hearing Chad Lawson's pianistic piece under the same title "I wandered lonely as a cloud" served as an inspiration for this poem.

I wandered lonely as a cloud,
Holding neither worth nor what to be proud,
Aimlessly sailing in a silvered blue sky,
Wishing instead I was awry.

I wished instead I was a balloon,
Up so high I could touch the moon,
I could count the stars and maybe see a planet,
Perhaps even try to catch them with a magnet.

I wished instead I had wings to fly,
Maybe as a bird, an airplane or a butterfly,
Spread my arms open and visit many places,
Move freely around and see plenty of faces.

I wished instead I was a kite,
With lots of shapes and colors,
Oh my, what a sight,
To be held by the hands of children as a toy,
Play and laugh aloud with them, what a joy.

I wished instead I was a gust of wind,
Make a loud sound and never be seen,
I would be really powerful and immensely
fierce,
Strong enough to whistle, howl and pierce.

I wished instead I was a starbright,
Shining and sparkling to lighten the night,
A big or small stone, easy to carry in a pocket,
Likely the body part of a comet.

I wished so hard, wished my heart away,
A simple lonely cloud no longer to stay,
The heaviness of my sorrow made me change
my form,
I became gray with anger and created a storm.

I never imagined having such a power,
A little cloud like me to destroy and devour,
This ugliness that upheld it wasn't my true
nature,
This was someone else, an intruder, a stranger.

Then, I only wished for the tempest to stop,
The cyclone, the typhoon for a little cloud to
swap,
But it can only be achieved by loving myself
more,
A wandering lonely cloud as I was before.

Friday, March 8th, 2024

I want to dive deep into your quietness,
so that you will not be lonely in your solitude.

– E. N. Gavani

Friday, April 19th, 2024

Blooming like a daffodil

Commemorating the vernal equinox of March 20th, 2024.

What a joy when spring shows up at the door,
When you see greenery everywhere and colors
galore,
Such little things that make your heart feel full,
Like the smell of beaded dew on a full moon.

Such a wonder to see the springs awakening,
Watch the waltz of the icing rivers melting,
Hear the nature sing your favorite lullaby,
Stretch your arms with the trees reaching for the
sky.

What I like the most is waking up at dawn,
Right before you hear the nature's stirred yawn,
Think about what treasures the day ahead will
hide,
Wait with the camellias as they beckon the sun
to rise.

Such delights lay on earth all around,
Vast beauty everywhere in everything to be
found,
The wisdom of solitude coming back each
spring,
And blooming in my heart like a daffodil.

Wednesday, March 20th, 2024

Unhealed child

The perfection in the imperfections.
The words in between the lines.
The insecurities behind the confident smiles.
The truth that rests beneath the lies.
These are the things I look out for.
The unhealed child inside each one of us.
Cradling alone on the cold floor.

Monday, April 15th, 2024

Caterpillars dancing in the wind

Do you ever dream or reminisce,
Of a bygone place,
a day of bliss?
A moment stuck in time,
An instant back to go,
Revive what has been lost,
Find out what went amiss.

Do you ever wonder,
in a reverie,
Where your childhood memories,
now got to be.
Sweet memories of summer yore,
Buried in the depths of the sea,
Hiding beneath the sandcastles,
That you built so dearly.

How do you uncover the bearings,
That spot in the evergreen,
Dandelions blown away in wishes,
Playing catch in the stream?
That musky smell of earth,
A landscape so serene,
Watching caterpillars,
dancing in the wind.

Do your icy veins,
ever have that longing,
Of the warmth of the sun,
And the birds calling.
Forgetting the freezing cold
of the present age,
Letting the soul run free,
From the golden cage.
Far from everything,
the slightest of worries,
Away from idle chatter,
and all human wronging.

Sunday, March 10th, 2024

Prayer

I pray they get to know You, my Lord,
Reside in Your mercy when this world breaks
their heart,
Help me teach them the greatness of Your word,
Give them eyes to see the blessings around.

Teach them the language of water, my God,
How it brings joy and music with each passing
flow,
No matter its shape, how high or low it runs,
Be deep like still water and learn to let go.

Teach them the language of seeds, my God,
That it doesn't matter if you're big or small,
At times we have to stay buried deep in the dark,
But only through believing, into flowers we will
grow.

Teach them the language of leaves, my God,
How to embrace change and still have hope,
We will have to battle many cruel winters,
But the chanting of spring will make it all
worthy.

Teach them the language of earth, my God,
How to be grounded, heartily give and heal,
How Your presence is found in each grain of
soil,
How working the dirt will help them bring You
near.

Teach them the language of shadows, my God,
The balances of this sphere where they coexist,
For there will be no shadow if there were no
light,
How good and bad, black, and white intertwist.

I pray they get to know You, my Lord,
Help me teach them the path of Light,
Show them how they can reach the unreachable,
By praising and worshiping the one and only
God.

Wednesday, March 13th, 2024

Strings of the Heart

Every morning, a single kiss escapes the corners
of my thoughts,
and comes to wish you a good morning.

– E. N. Gavani

Thursday, April 18th, 2024

My promise

I'm sorry I can't dance any longer,
I used to enjoy grooving to the beat,
But the burden of the days consumed my spirit,
And now I'm left with two left feet.

I'm sorry I can't drink either,
I can't seem to put down an alcoholic shot,
But if you are up to slower moments,
Perhaps I can brew some tea in a pot.

I'm sorry you didn't find a friend in me,
Someone to go out to explore the wild,
I always knew you liked an adventure,
But never presumed I wasn't on a par.

I'm sorry I'm not a good companion,
I always thought I would be a good partner in
crime,
But it seems you and I are on a different
vibration,
Even though we've been together for a lifetime.

I'm sorry I'm not what you thought of me,
I can't live up to the expectations,
I wish I became what you wanted me to be,
Instead, I'm just plain without sensations.

I'm sorry I'm basic, and not fabulous or fun,
But at least I'm honest and never lie,
I hope what I offer can be equally enough,
A promise to be faithful and love you till I die.

Sunday, March 10th, 2024

The meaning of love

To love someone, it means to slowly die,
Pack your own bags and kiss yourself goodbye,
The journey of loving will transform you and
change,
The world as you know it will come to an end.

It will gradually happen, you will barely feel it,
One can only hope that for the better they'll
mutate,
For into something ugly you can also convert,
Yourself at the end totally to alienate.

Loving someone means walking jointly in the
same pace,
Never letting go of each other's hand,
If either one falls behind or moves ahead,
Both will suffer a silent path.

Tuesday, March 19th, 2024

Red rose

I love flowers, - she said shyly.
But not big bouquets.
Just a single stem will do.
A single stem of flower it's what really says:
"This flower is for you,
Just because I love you"
So, he took a vow to bring her a single stem
of red rose every day.
Even after the day she left and passed away.
And after he joined her for eternity too,
A red rose was placed each day on her tomb.
As a message to his lover,
that his love for her was eternally true.

Thursday, April 18th, 2024

Paradox of love

Love does not obey anyone,
It never plays by any rules.
It brings our riches to the ground,
And gives us wealth when we are poor.
Love ages us while we are young,
And gives us youth when we are old.
It spreads its wings to fly up high,
While we try so hard to make it root.

Sunday, April 14th, 2024

Voice in the wind

- For the ones in a long-distance relationship

I heard your voice in the wind,
Whispering sweet names,
Into my tired lonely ears.
So, I opened my arms,
In a receiving embrace,
And all of a sudden,
I felt your breath on my face.
All the sudden,
I smelled the sweat of your skin,
I felt your warmth in mine,
And the sound of your grin.
The caress of your fingers,
On my long ebony hair,
Tantalizing with lustful desires,
Teasing and flirting afar in the air.
And then the wind becomes you,
And you become the wind,
Swaying, twisting, waltzing me,
In a whirl of sensual dance,
Encircling me with such ardor,
Daring to breathe I have no chance.

And next thing I know,
I have become the wind,
And the wind has become I,
And all that we are,
All that has become,
Is a hurricane of carnal affection,
Into which we have succumbed.

Sunday, April 14th, 2024

And then the wind becomes you,
and you become the wind.
Swaying, twisting, waltzing me,
In a whirl of sensual dance,
Encircling me with such ardor,
Daring to breathe I have no chance.
– E. N. Gavani

He/ She might be to whomever dreams and
hopes to have him/her, but in my heart he/she is
only mine.

– E. N. Gavani

Wednesday, April 17th, 2024

And I loved him/her so

And I loved him/her so.
Like you love a rare creature
You admire from afar,
never getting too close
From fearing you will scare it away.
Like you love a beautiful flower
That you water every day,
never thinking of picking it.
Like you love the most precious possession,
never daring to behold for too long,
from fearing you will break it in pieces.
I loved him/her so.
A love he/she will never know.
Gently.
Softly.
Fiercely.

Wednesday. April 17th, 2024

Transcending love

We will meet again somewhere one day.
This is not our final goodbye.
Time will have changed both of us such,
We won't recognize our physical forms much.
But I will know you by your smile,
I will know you by your gaze,
I will find you by your gait,
Through lifetimes of endless maze.
I will know you like you have been mine,
Always and every day,
The strings of our hearts entwined,
Forever and a day.

Tuesday, April 16th, 2024

Deditio

Waiting to hear the footprints,
that imprinted within me,
The burning, the longing, the agony,
that refuses to set me free.

Mine is the desire,
to kiss the earth you touch,
For a stupid fool like me,
wanting more would be too much.

This yearning I possess,
it puts my sanity to the test.
There are no more days, neither time nor clock,
to measure the thoughts of you that over flock.

Into your ivory chest,
like a bird I want to nest,
Till I build that course, that path,
I shall never find any rest.

A hundred flowers I will sow,
to taste the sweetest of nectars.
Thousand candles will pray to the sky,
For me to be your sole protector.

Oh, my sweet fair sorceress,
what sort of spell did you cast?
What kind of bewitchment is this,
with such powers that over last?

From the mystery of your aura,
I would never want to wake,
I surrender entirely to you my love,
into the soulless eternal ache.

Friday, February 29th, 2024

You can **Fail** in love just as easily as you can **Fall** in love.
Learn how to understand the signs and the languages of both.

– E. N. Gavani

Thursday, April 18th, 2024

Failing in love

He failed to understand how she needed to be
touched,
She failed to realize the ways he loved her so
much.

She failed to see what he wanted to feel seen,
He failed to hear how her love lay in words in
between.

They both failed to comprehend how one loved
the other so,
Love passing by concealed, hearts slowly
covering in snow.

And such true love got lost without a single
track,
Lovers forever plagued, without a trail to meet
back.

Wednesday, March 17th, 2024

Two ships passing in the night

I am here, and you are there,
Wondering how things will come to be,
For two ships like us passing in the night,
Slowly, quietly drifting into a lonely sea.

Thursday, April 18th, 2024

The woodwinds
Ode to loss, life, and love

Nothing really ends, it simply changes form.
Bear this thought in mind, and you'll find out,
that nothing is truly lost or gone.

- E. N. Gavani

Friday, April 19th, 2024

Image in the sky

In loving memory of my grandma gone too soon.

Oftentimes, I think of you looking up at the sky,
Wondering if I would be able to find you up
there,
A sign, a signal, a message to descry,
Perhaps a little kiss blown in the air.

I often search for you in a ray of sun,
Wishing to pull you out from a single cloud,
In hope to catch your smile and beg you to stay.
Tell you how difficult it has been since we've
been apart.

I often look for you in the looking glass,
Staring intensely at my own reflection,
Will I resemble you as the years pass?
A creature of beauty carved into perfection.

I was merely a child when God sent for you,
Leaving a void to fill in place of your loving
embrace,
I was forced to remember you for longer than I
knew you,
And gained a heavenly angel to watch over me
instead.

Saturday, March 16th, 2024

I often look for you in the looking glass,
Staring intensely at my own reflection,
Will I resemble you as the years pass?
A creature of beauty carved into perfection.

- E. N. Gavani

Love happened first

To Fred and Frank.
And all the dear ones I had to say goodbye to.

Bidding farewell to a loved one it's never easy,
No matter how young or old you grow,
It shatters your heart in a thousand pieces,
Each piece must learn now beating on their own.

Saying goodbye, it will always hurt,
Missing them each day piercing even more,
You're left to breathe with only one lung,
No strength to move or carry on.

Letting go it's such a hard thing to do,
Paralyzed, defeated, no more dreams to chase,
The ache, the regret, the resentment, the loss,
A rollercoaster of feelings marching down the
road.

But then a bluejay's feather falls at your feet,
You see a butterfly or simply listen to a song,
And all the sudden your heart remembers and
falls in peace,
It was love that happened first for you to feel the
loss.

Thursday, March 21st, 2024

Better let the pain sit through

No use to keep on fighting it,
Better let the pain sit through,
Make room for it in your heart,
And let it conquer each inch of you.

No use in trying to push it out,
Better let its powers soar high,
Nobody will give you a sterling medal,
For sealing the corners of your eyes dry.

No use in concealing it tight, I tell you,
But you can give it a try if you must,
The torment will be too much to bear and
endure,
Like the pressure in a kettle, it's meant to burst
and blast.

You can try pulling out the weeds too,
Extract the garden from every draining withered
thought,
But that will be just a superficial adjustment,
For the worms still lie in you deep down.

No use to keep on lying about it,
The intruder is now a guest in your own house,
Better pull out a chair and offer a glass,
You'll find no praise in letting him starve.

Better set the table and feed him up,
Tell him all that's been hiding in your broken
heart,
Maybe you'll find a way to live better together,
After satisfying his large appetite.

No use in resisting it,
Now pain is an essential part of you,
For once it possesses all your belongings,
You must start learning to live in two.

Saturday, March 16th, 2024

Always remember

To my children (Version 2)

Learn to forgive it all, my love,
Don't let resentment sink you down,
The weight can pluck your plumes apart,
Mark your angelic face with a frown.

Learn to love fearlessly, my heart,
Even when bones got tired and strength is gone,
For love heals all the deepest scars,
Let kindness lead forevermore.

Learn to speak softly, my child,
For words have powers beyond unseen,
When a broken soul in your path you'll find,
Lend them a spark of your gleam.

Never lose the child in you, my dear,
Let your heart be feather-light,
Don't permit this world instill you fear,
Always keep God's truth in sight.

Always remember where you come from, my
cherubs,
Remember your roots, remember your dreams,
You are my sons, an image of Heavens,
Rule your lives as kings and queens.

Wednesday, March 6th, 2024

The day I'm gone

To my children (version 1)

I will forever be with you, my child,
You will always carry me with you,
I've loved your little heart through and through,
With such love I've never thought it to be true.

You will always be mine to keep, my cub.
My pride, my love, my life, my heart,
Watching you grow it's such bittersweet,
Nothing can break our bond apart.

I will always hold you a little tighter,
Though my grip will loosen in time,
But you must be strong, my little fighter,
For one day I'll be gone but never forgotten.

As long as you search for me, my sweets,
You will always find me there,
I'll reach to you through winds, through dreams,
We will still have plenty of things to share.

I would have to leave you one day, my boy,
The thought of it makes my soul ache,
But I pray I leave your heart with joy,
Don't spend your days in dark despair.

You've been the most precious of gifts, my
beloved,
My light, my anchor, my truest blessing,
My time on earth is a zenith indeed,
The moment you came, I stopped my questing.

I will forever be with you, my child,
You will always carry me with you,
I've loved your little heart through and through,
With such love I've never thought it to be true.

Wednesday, March 6th, 2024

For mom

I heard God's laughter,
through your laughter,
Saw the sun rays,
through your golden locks,
My world had the colors of
your sparkling hazel eyes,
My heart followed yours.
without asking any whys.
Your faery steps lead mine,
into dreamy cruises,
Your words were the salve,
soothing cuts and bruises.
The fragrant heather honey,
cannot rival your scent,
Just an instant embracing you,
is a lifetime in heaven spent.
However far or big I go,
I will still need your motherly touch,
Holding my hand and reaching my heart,
Without ever saying too much.
I was a little girl then,
I'm still even littler today,
To my children I want to show and tell,
How a motherly love will always stay.

To my children I want to show and teach,
The beauty your brittle hands drew,
Although tempests and struggles overreached,
Your love taught me how to make it through.
I was a little girl yesterday,
Still the littlest today,
To stay your little girl the longest,
To heavenly Father each night will pray.

Friday, March 15th, 2024

She wears her femininity
like the night sky wears the stars,
not for the world to hold
but for herself, to know she is never empty
For herself to feel whole.

– E. N. Gavani

A pocketful of stars

I have a handful of stars,
Deep in the blue jeans of my pocket,
To brighten the skies when luster is dearth,
Toss them in the air into the milky way orbit.

I have a skyful of yesteryear,
That I will forever hold dearly tight,
A pocketful of gleam and sheer,
To shine a lesson into today's world light.

I have a pocketful of stars,
For when the days are dark and gray,
A pocketful of laughter and joy,
A handful of blessings to get me by the day.

I have a pocketful of glitter,
That the star-man in the sky gave to me,
With the promise to spread around the spark,
And share with others to help them see.

I have a pocketful of wisdom,
Learnt through mistakes and heartache,
But traded instead for something beautiful,
Away from resentment and heartbreak.

Saturday, April 6th, 2024

The Brass Trumpet of resilience and perseverance

Do not open the door to your heart to everyone
who knocks on it.

                    – E. N. Gavani

Of the sleepless nights

I've told you a million times,
Please do not interrupt my sleep.
For in my sleep I want no disturbances,
And your presence makes me weep.

A million times I've told you,
Please do not appear in my dream.
For in my dreams only I can make room,
To welcome whom, I most esteem.

How many times do I have to say it?
But you still don't want to listen,
You are a spiritual gangster at heart,
And it seems you're on a mission.

You should know I have changed,
And I have no use for you no more.
You're merely a ghost I remembered,
Walking outside the door.

So, mark my word one final time,
And arrest your attempts of divine redemption,
For what you have said and done before,
Leave no room for restoration.

Wednesday, April 26th, 2023

My unanswered questions

I always wonder what it is like,
to see me through your eyes,
Whether my soft being still remains,
the most beautiful of sights?

That way I would know the reason,
behind your constant winding flees,
Unceasingly chasing,
the next shimmering sparkling things.

I wonder if your presence,
for mine longs away,
With every minute and heartbeat,
of the passing day.

What earthy solace of the flesh,
does your body seek,
when my snowy skin,
is out of your reach?

The aches and sorrows,
you must endure,
to taste the kiss,
of my love so pure?

I wish I could warn you,
dear lover of mine,
Deception lies within,
pretty trinkets that shine.

The worldly turmoil,
have neither start nor end,
for the one who likes to meander,
my lover and friend.

The soul yearns,
for the eternal divine truth,
behind the blinding veil,
of the unfathomable youth.

Alas, you choose to trade,
a precious stone to pebbles,
Maybe I will find more success,
into writing fables.

Wednesday, February 26th, 2024

I have never seen anything more powerful than a
woman who gathers up her strength and tears, to
wipe away her own pain and fears, and walk again
in a path that her eyes washed and blessed anew.

– E. N. Gavani

Monday, April 15th, 2024

Rebellion

I want to leave, run away.
Disappear in thin air.
Far from everything,
And everyone I know.
Find a spot to hide,
Protect my own truth,
If such a place exists,
Even farther I want to go.

I want to cry out.
Melt the pain.
Scream aloud the silenced tears.
Drops of blood drowning inside,
In the vessel oppressed by the years.
Is there such a hole,
A profound dark sea,
Somewhere to pour out the soul-ache,
If such a place truly exists,
Even deeper the bitterness,
I want to take.

I want to destroy,
Tear apart the masks,
This cynical world
Changes each day,
By showing your colors
And a blunt face nowadays,
It means to live in great dismay.
I want to smash,
Break apart the lies,
Disfiguring the justice that once ruled,
Leash out the anger of a million voices,
This crazed haze once had them fooled.

I want to light a fire,
burn it all to the ground,
Let heavy rains wash off the ashes,
Send for a wind-whirling hurricane through,
To erase even the slightest of traces.
I want to wipe it all clean,
Like in the myth of the great flood,
Built an arc for the good-hearted few,
Then submerge small and big cities down.
Might be the only way to be salvaged from,
masquerade balls with balloons and clowns.

Saturday, March 16th, 2024

Love/Hate to death

The fault lies in me,
I am to blame,
I am the sole reason,
My pride is not the same.
The wrongdoing is all mine,
You weren't even part of the play.
It was utterly foolish of me,
Any reason to disobey.
A skeleton I fancied, a skeleton.
Merely a pack of bones.
Dressed and designed his robes,
Even sewed them on my own.
Embroidered traits and virtues,
To match the body and face,
Damned be those romance novels,
That initiated such a disgrace.
I fell for a skeleton slowly,
Towards a black hole gravitating,
I sacrificed all the planets and stars,
That I had been so carefully curating.
Cursed be that doomed day,
When my eyes met your soulless socket-gaze,
And whatever time was spent thereafter,
That made me the object of your funs and
games.

Undressing you from all that scam,
I realized you were simply a naked fraud,
That I naively had concocted,
Into making myself an idiot.
It was all my fault, so you see,
But I've forgiven you anyway,
A bouquet of roses as truce I bring,
For your filthy bones in peaceful rest to stay.

Sunday, March 17th, 2024

Sometimes, we fall for the beautifully painted
picture in our minds, only to realize it's framed in
the gallery of our imagination, not in the halls of
our reality.

- E. N. Gavani

I am Gavan

Gavan it's a name of Welsh and Scottish origins meaning "White falcon/hawk" or "Hawk of the battle." The origin of this name served as the inspiration for this poem.

I will rise from deep,
Through the endless of times,
Appear from nothingness into thin air,
I've been a servant of pagan savages,
For such long,
I am a hawk of battle beyond compare.
Those who try to put me in darkness,
Into darkness I will see them disappear.
Sharpen your knives, you dirty scoundrels,
I won't be showing any doubt or fear.
I am bred in bloody honor,
A moon-soldier built in silver flame,
After I am completely through with you,
Rest assured I will still mark your grave.
Send for demons, giants, vultures, and beasts,
Let all hell run loose and free,
Try your bestest, I dare you crones,
You will only awaken the devil in me.
Through the fog of memories,
Through all the dirt and heavy smoke,
As a phoenix I will rise my blood avenging.

You'll watch me soaring high above.
You thought you'd be my end, but you were my awakening.
No matter what you put me through,
Break my wings with the sharpest stone,
I am Gavan, take a good look at me,
By my honor I will not be forlorn.
Pluck my skin, disfigure my form,
Even indulge yourself in some dark magic,
I am Gavan, a white protector,
My call for the skies will not be ignored.
You've exhausted all sources,
you poor crooks,
Now you're resorting to mudding my name,
I am Gavan, the white hawk,
The words from your mouths will not bring me shame.
I am Gavan, the white falcon,
Remember this much and never forget,
I am Gavan, have a final look,
My bloodline and yours are not the same.

Wednesday, March 20th, 2024

Born of a spirit too wild to tame,
Desire for freedom bursting like a flame,
A force so powerful, no one can frame.

– E. N. Gavani

Don't fret over might have been's

Don't fret over might have been's,
Don't lose your sleep over what if's,
Rest your head peacefully on the pillow,
And rejoice in the present that God gives.

Don't get lost on opening doors to the past,
Don't exhaust your mind in regrets,
Don't overthink,
You will drown in the river of melancholia
running backwards,
While time and life won't wait for you still.

Take each season and moment as it comes,
Each hill and valley has a precious gift to bear,
If mountains looked back glooming over their
shapes,
There would be no peaks to climb,
A scarce on nature's wisdom to share.

Monday, April 29th, 2024

Dare to love yourself unapologetically

Dare to love yourself unapologetically,
You will never be,
As young,
As beautiful,
As energetic,
As you are today,
At this moment in time.
When time has passed cruelly,
For most cruel it can be,
And you find a few more worry lines,
In your portrait,
In your bones,
In your hair,
In your skin,
The worst regret you will feel,
Would be not having,
Laughed more,
Loved more.

So take the courage,
Embrace your body,
Rejoice in your sensuality,
Get sultry,
Feel sexy,
Dance in the rain,
Smile at strangers,
Let the wind run free in your hair,
Let the sun draw freckles on your skin,
You owe it to yourself,
And all the women before you,
So I dare you,
Dare yourself,
Love your own,
Unapologetically,
The time is now.

Sunday, April 14th, 2024

Learn to love yourself unapologetically.
Dance in the rain,
Smile at strangers,
Let the wind run free in your hair,
Let the sun draw freckles on your skin,
You owe it to yourself,
And all the women before you.

- E. N. Gavani

Epilogue

Your life can really be a succession of lives.
We die from pain and are born through love,
numerous times within a lifetime.
It is the intensity of each rebirth,
the reason behind each pain.
The heart will play all the notes of the
pentagram,
until symphony will become its name.

– E. N. Gavani
Wednesday, May 1st, 2024

A little taste of what's soon to come from this author

Fire and bloom

She is a dance,
Between both fire and bloom.
Drawing her strength,
From both the sun and the moon.
Her elements rooted deep,
In forests of trees,
Like a baby in a mother's womb.

– E. N. Gavani